SOCIAL PROGRESS AND SUSTAINABILITY
Shelter • Safety • Literacy • Health • Freedom • Environment

NEAR EAST

Foreword by **Michael Green,**
Executive Director, Social Progress Imperative

By Don Rauf

SOCIAL PROGRESS AND SUSTAINABILITY

SOCIAL PROGRESS AND SUSTAINABILITY

Shelter • Safety • Literacy • Health • Freedom • Environment

NEAR EAST

Don Rauf

Foreword by
Michael Green
Executive Director, Social Progress Imperative

MASON CREST

Mason Crest
450 Parkway Drive, Suite D
Broomall, PA 19008
www.masoncrest.com

Printed and bound in the United States of America

First printing
9 8 7 6 5 4 3 2 1

Series ISBN: 978-1-4222-3490-7
Hardcover ISBN: 978-1-4222-3497-6
ebook ISBN: 978-1-4222-8392-9

Library of Congress Cataloging-in-Publication Data

Names: Rauf, Don, author.
Title: Near East/by Don Rauf; foreword by Michael Green, executive director, Social Progress Imperative.
Description: Broomall, PA : Mason Crest, [2017] | Series: Social progress and sustainability | Includes index.
Identifiers: LCCN 2016007608| ISBN 9781422234976 (hardback) | ISBN 9781422234907 (series) | ISBN 9781422283929 (ebook)
Subjects: LCSH: Social indicators—Middle East—Juvenile literature. | Middle East—Social conditions—Juvenile literature. | Middle East—Economic conditions—Juvenile literature.
Classification: LCC HN656.A85 R38 2017 | DDC 306.0956—dc23
LC record available at http://lccn.loc.gov/2016007608

Developed and Produced by Print Matters Productions, Inc. (www.printmattersinc.com)

Project Editor: David Andrews
Design: Bill Madrid, Madrid Design
Copy Editor: Laura Daly

Note on Statistics:
All social progress statistics, except where noted, are used by courtesy of the Social Progress Imperative and reflect 2015 ratings.

CONTENTS

KEY ICONS TO LOOK FOR:

Text-Dependent Questions: These questions send readers back to the text for more careful attention to the evidence presented there.

Words to Understand: These words with their easy-to-understand definitions will increase readers' understanding of the text while building vocabulary skills.

Series Glossary of Key Terms: This back-of-the-book glossary contains terminology used throughout this series. Words found here increase readers' ability to read and comprehend higher-level books and articles in this field.

Research Projects: Readers are pointed toward areas of further inquiry connected to each chapter. Suggestions are provided for projects that encourage deeper research and analysis.

Sidebars: This boxed material within the main text allows readers to build knowledge, gain insights, explore possibilities, and broaden their perspectives by weaving together additional information to provide realistic and holistic perspectives.

SOCIAL PROGRESS AROUND THE GLOBE

Michael Green

How do you measure the success of a country? It's not as easy as you might think. Americans are used to thinking of their country as the best in the world, but what does "best" actually mean? For a long time, the United States performed better than any other country in terms of the sheer size of its economy, and bigger was considered better. Yet China caught up with the United States in 2014 and now has a larger overall economy.

What about average wealth? The United States does far better than China here but not as well as several countries in Europe and the Middle East.

Most of us would like to be richer, but is money really what we care about? Is wealth really how we want to measure the success of countries—or cities, neighborhoods, families, and individuals? Would you really want to be rich if it meant not having access to the World Wide Web, or suffering a painful disease, or not being safe when you walked near your home?

Using money to compare societies has a long history, including the invention in the 1930s of an economic measurement called gross domestic product (GDP). Basically, GDP for the United States "measures the output of goods and services produced by labor and property located within the U.S. during a given time period." The concept of GDP was actually created by the economist Simon Kuznets for use by the federal government. Using measures like GDP to guide national economic policies helped pull the United States out of the Great Depression and helped Europe and Japan recover after World War II. As they say in business school, if you can measure it, you can manage it.

Many positive activities contribute to GDP, such as
- Building schools and roads
- Growing crops and raising livestock
- Providing medical care

More and more experts, however, are seeing that we may need another way to measure the success of a nation.

Other kinds of activities increase a country's GDP, but are these signs that a country is moving in a positive direction?
- Building and maintaining larger prisons for more inmates
- Cleaning up after hurricanes or other natural disasters
- Buying alcohol and illegal drugs
- Maintaining ecologically unsustainable use of water, harvesting of trees, or catching of fish

GDP also does not address inequality. A few people could become extraordinarily wealthy, while the rest of a country is plunged into poverty and hunger, but this wouldn't be reflected in the GDP.

In the turbulent 1960s, Robert F. Kennedy, the attorney general of the United States and brother of President John F. Kennedy, famously said of GDP during a 1968 address to students at the University of Kansas: "It counts napalm and counts nuclear warheads and armored cars for the police to fight the riots in our cities ... [but] the gross national product does not allow for the health of our children. ... [I]t measures everything in short, except that which makes life worthwhile."

For countries like the United States that already have large or strong economies, it is not clear that simply making the economy larger will improve human welfare. Developed countries struggle with issues like obesity, diabetes, crime, and environmental challenges. Increasingly, even poorer countries are struggling with these same issues.

Noting the difficulties that many countries experience as they grow wealthier (such as increased crime and obesity), people around the world have begun to wonder: What if we measure the things we really care about directly, rather than assuming that greater GDP will mean improvement in everything we care about? Is that even possible?

The good news is that it is. There is a new way to think about prosperity, one that does not depend on measuring economic activity using traditional tools like GDP.

Advocates of the "Beyond GDP" movement, people ranging from university professors to leaders of businesses, from politicians to religious leaders, are calling for more attention to directly measuring things we all care about, such as hunger, homelessness, disease, and unsafe water.

One of the new tools that has been developed is called the Social Progress Index (SPI), and it is the data from this index that is featured in this series of books, Social Progress and Sustainability.

The SPI has been created to measure and advance social progress outcomes at a fine level of detail in communities of different sizes and at different levels of wealth. This means that we can compare the performance of very different countries using one standard set of measurements, to get a sense of how well different countries perform compared to each other. The index measures how the different parts of society, including governments, businesses, not-for-profits, social entrepreneurs, universities, and colleges, work together to improve human welfare. Similarly, it does not strictly measure the actions taken in a particular place. Instead, it measures the outcomes in a place.

The SPI begins by defining what it means to be a good society, structured around three fundamental themes:

- Do people have the basic needs for survival: food, water, shelter, and safety?
- Do people have the building blocks of a better future: education, information, health, and sustainable ecosystems?

- Do people have a chance to fulfill their dreams and aspirations by having rights and freedom of choice, without discrimination, with access to the cutting edge of human knowledge?

The Social Progress Index is published each year, using the best available data for all the countries covered. You can explore the data on our website at http://socialprogressimperative.org. The data for this series of books is from our 2015 index, which covered 133 countries. Countries that do not appear in the 2015 index did not have the right data available to be included.

A few examples will help illustrate how overall Social Progress Index scores compare to measures of economic productivity (for example, GDP per capita), and also how countries can differ on specific lenses of social performance.

- The United States (6th for GDP per capita, 16th for SPI overall) ranks 6th for Shelter but 68th in Health and Wellness, because of factors such as obesity and death from heart disease.
- South Africa (62nd for GDP per capita, 63rd for SPI) ranks 44th in Access to Information and Communications but only 114th in Health and Wellness, because of factors such as relatively short life expectancy and obesity.
- India (93rd for GDP per capita, 101st for SPI) ranks 70th in Personal Rights but only 128th in Tolerance and Inclusion, because of factors such as low tolerance for different religions and low tolerance for homosexuals.
- China (66th for GDP per capita, 92nd for SPI) ranks 58th in Shelter but 84th in Water and Sanitation, because of factors such as access to piped water.
- Brazil (55th for GDP per capita, 42nd for SPI) ranks 61st in Nutrition and Basic Medical Care but only 122nd in Personal Safety, because of factors such as a high homicide rate.

The Social Progress Index focuses on outcomes. Politicians can boast that the government has spent millions on feeding the hungry; the SPI measures how well fed people really are. Businesses can boast investing money in their operations or how many hours their employees have volunteered in the community; the SPI measures actual literacy rates and access to the Internet. Legislators and administrators might focus on how much a country spends on health care; the SPI measures how long and how healthily people live. The index doesn't measure whether countries have passed laws against discrimination; it measures whether people experience discrimination. And so on.

- What if your family measured its success only by the amount of money it brought in but ignored the health and education of members of the family?
- What if a neighborhood focused only on the happiness of the majority while discriminating against one family because they were different?
- What if a country focused on building fast cars but was unable to provide clean water and air?

The Social Progress Index can also be adapted to measure human well-being in areas smaller than a whole country.

- A Social Progress Index for the Amazon region of Brazil, home to 24 million people and covering one of the world's most precious environmental assets, shows how 800 different municipalities compare. A map of that region shows where needs are greatest and is informing a development strategy for the region that balances the interests of people and the planet. Nonprofits, businesses, and governments in Brazil are now using this data to improve the lives of the people living in the Amazon region.
- The European Commission—the governmental body that manages the European Union—is using the Social Progress Index to compare the performance of multiple regions in each of 28 countries and to inform development strategies.
- We envision a future where the Social Progress Index will be used by communities of different sizes around the world to measure how well they are performing and to help guide governments, businesses, and nonprofits to make better choices about what they focus on improving, including learning lessons from other communities of similar size and wealth that may be performing better on some fronts. Even in the United States subnational social progress indexes are underway to help direct equitable growth for communities.

The Social Progress Index is intended to be used along with economic measurements such as GDP, which have been effective in guiding decisions that have lifted hundreds of millions of people out of abject poverty. But it is designed to let countries go even further, not just making economies larger but helping them devote resources to where they will improve social progress the most. The vision of my organization, the Social Progress Imperative, which created the Social Progress Index, is that in the future the Social Progress Index will be considered alongside GDP when people make decisions about how to invest money and time.

Imagine if we could measure what charities and volunteers really contribute to our societies. Imagine if businesses competed based on their whole contribution to society—not just economic, but social and environmental. Imagine if our politicians were held accountable for how much they made people's lives better, in real, tangible ways. Imagine if everyone, everywhere, woke up thinking about how their community performed on social progress and about what they could do to make it better.

Note on Text:
While Michael Green wrote the foreword and data is from the 2015 Social Progress Index, the rest of the text is not by Michael Green or the Social Progress Imperative.

This political map shows the countries of the region discussed in this book.

SOCIAL PROGRESS IN THE NEAR EAST

The Near East is a land of extremes. It has extreme heat. It has extreme religious divisions. In one country there, people earn the most in the world—Qatar has an annual GDP (gross domestic product) per capita of $143,400. But the Near East also has a country with one of the lowest GDPs in the world—Yemen, where it is $3,800 per year. Yet money does not tell the whole story when it comes to measuring social progress and the health and well-being of citizens.

This volume explores the level of social progress in the countries that make up the Near East: Bahrain, Iran, Iraq, Israel, Jordan, Kuwait, Lebanon, Oman, Qatar, Saudi Arabia, Syria, the United Arab Emirates, and Yemen. (For the purposes of this book, Palestine is not included because not enough data were available to rank it in the Social Progress Index.) Social progress is a society's ability to meet the basic human needs of its citizens, create the building blocks that individuals and communities use to improve the quality of their lives, and make it possible for everyone to reach their potential. The book examines bare necessities, such as people's access to food, water, shelter, and basic medical care; it also considers whether people are safe, receive education, and enjoy personal freedom. It considers as well the political and natural environment.

To understand how social progress differs from one country to another, the Social Progress Imperative scored 133 countries around the world in three main areas:

Basic Human Needs: *Does a country provide for its people's most essential needs?*

Foundations of Well-being: *Are the building blocks in place for individuals and communities to enhance and sustain well-being?*

Opportunity: *Is there opportunity for all individuals to reach their full potential?*

Based on dozens of scores in these three areas, the Social Progress Imperative calculated an overall Social Progress Index (SPI) score for each country. Scores were then classified into six groups, from very low social progress to very high. Actual scores for countries in the Near East can be found in Chapter 4. Countries around the world are using SPI scores and rankings to identify areas for improvement and to help guide social investment.

What Is the Near East?

The origin of the word "east" comes from Sanskrit, which is one of the world's most ancient languages. "East" developed from the Sanskrit *ushas*, which means "dawn." Ushas is also the goddess of the dawn. She rides a golden chariot on her path across the sky, warding off evil spirits of the night. The word makes sense because the sun rises in the east. Western cultures adopted the terms "Near East" and "Far East" to distinguish between countries in eastern

Asia and those located in western Asia. The British started these two simple geographic labels—countries are either "Near" or "Far." Today, the Near East may refer to many countries that also comprise the Middle East, and the Middle East is often used to refer to most of the area that is the Near East. (Although Turkey is sometimes considered Near Eastern as well, it's at a crossroads between the East and West, so some view the nation as part of Europe or Eurasia. This series includes Turkey as part of Eurasia.)

Visitors in the Arab market of the Old City of Jerusalem, Israel, the most visited city in the country, with 3.5 million tourists annually.

Because most of the governments here are still basically monarchies that greatly limit personal freedoms, the Near East overall doesn't get very high marks on the Social Progress Index. The countries that are aligned with Western ideals—at least to some degree—seem to fare better than those that are opposed to the West. Israel, a longtime ally of the United States, earns a 72.6 rating on the SPI. For some of the countries in the region, large deposits of oil have made them incredibly wealthy. As the nation that exports the most petroleum of any in the world, Saudi Arabia is one of the richest countries in the Near East and is a traditional friend of the West and the United States. The country scores 64.27 on the SPI. Saudi Arabia has a powerful military that has helped to maintain some stability in the region, but strict enforcement and interpretation of Islamic law has led to harsh treatment of individuals. Those caught with alcohol, for example, may receive 100 lashes as punishment, and drug offenses may be punishable by beheading. Kuwait is also oil-rich and a friend of the West. It ranks at 69.19 on the SPI, and the United Arab Emirates (UAE) ranks at just about the same level as the United States, with a 72.79.

Overall in this region, the UAE (39th), Israel (40th), and Kuwait (47th) get top scores on the SPI. The lowest scores are for Yemen (128th) and Iraq (113th). Bahrain, Libya, Oman, Qatar, and Syria do not have enough data for some of the components of the SPI, so their scores are not complete.

Just south of Saudi Arabia, Kuwait, and the UAE is Yemen, which has one of the lowest SPI scores in the region, at 40.30. Rebels took over the country at the beginning of 2015, and the government has a history of instability. With

Iran, the SPI is fairly low, at 56.82, although the country scores high when it comes to meeting basic human needs (78.42) and access to basic knowledge (91.89). Syria does not have a complete rating, but it has been the location of such uncertainty that it has performed low. Syria has been at the center of disruption—embroiled in a civil war and fighting against ISIS (the Islamic State of Iraq and the Levant, also called ISIL), designated as a terrorist organization by the United Nations (UN).

Located just to the north of Saudi Arabia, Syria and Iraq have both been living under the threat of ISIS, which formed in April 2013. It is a jihadist group, meaning that followers believe in creating an Islamic state governing all Muslims. Jihadists justify the use of violence to reach their goal. ISIS members are working to establish a caliphate (a form of Islamic government) that straddles Syria and Iraq. ISIS has ruled with great brutality, with regular

Russian fighter jets fly overhead. Russia engaged in air strikes in Syria.

torture and beheadings and other executions. The rule of ISIS has been described as a reign of terror. Those in power strictly enforce crimes against Islam as well, including smoking, alcohol consumption, and sex outside marriage. ISIS has been successful in taking over large parts of Syria and Iraq, including oil fields in Mosul in northern Iraq.

Saudi Arabia is an active member of the US-led anti-ISIS coalition. The coalition, including the United States, United Kingdom (UK), UAE, Turkey, and other countries, began air strikes against ISIS forces in Iraq in September 2014. In 2015 air strikes extended to ISIS-controlled areas in Syria. Although Saudi Arabia is too strong for ISIS to consider conquering, it may be an appealing target as the birthplace of Islam and a land rich in oil.

Even without ISIS, Syria has been in a state of civil war since 2011. In the spring of that year, protests against the government began, and President Bashar al-Assad responded with orders to the military to crush the opposition. These protests grew into a full-blown civil war in which more than 250,000 people are believed to have been killed. UN inspectors confirmed in 2013 that chemical weapons had been used against civilians but did not determine whether rebel or government forces were responsible. The US, the UK, France, and other countries supported the opposition groups. In 2015 Russia intervened in the civil war in support of President Assad and the government. A truce backed by the US and Russia to halt the fighting between the Syrian government and rebel groups began in late February 2016. It was hoped the truce would lead to peace talks.

The fighting in Syria led millions of people to flee, first to neighboring countries, then, beginning in 2015, to Europe. Since the beginning of the war, an estimated 11 million people have been forced from their homes in Syria, with about 4 million of them refugees in other countries.

Iraq currently has a fragile Islamic federal democracy in place. A civil war between Shiites and Sunnis (members of the two main branches of Islam) and Kurds (an ethnic group in northern Iraq, Turkey, and other countries) followed the US-led invasion of Iraq in 2003 to topple the country's leader, Saddam Hussein. The American presence in Iraq ended in 2011. The spillover of fighting from Syria and the continuing strength of ISIS are ongoing problems in the country.

A recent deal between Iran and an international group, led by the US, UK, France, Russia, China, and Germany, over Iran's development of nuclear power and weapons has led to the lifting of sanctions, or penalties, against it. An Islamic republic, Iran is becoming more progressive in many ways, with a more open economy and sharing of ideas. Perhaps unexpectedly, Iran is at the forefront of transgender surgery, family planning, and drug rehabilitation. A major reason for Western opposition to Iran in the past has been its stance against Israel, and many in leadership positions in Iran have been opposed to the United States.

Israel is prosperous, modern, and often a mired in conflict with its Arab neighbors. It was created in 1948 from the land called Palestine, which was part of Turkey before World War I, as a state for the spiritual, religious, and political identity of the Jewish people. Many Muslims felt this land should not be designated as a Jewish nation. Also, the holy city of Jerusalem, which is located in Israel, is sacred to both Muslims and Jews. The State of Palestine, which includes the West Bank, the Gaza Strip (or Gaza), and East Jerusalem, was first declared in 1988 and recognized as a nonmember observer state by the United Nations in 2012. (Due to gaps in statistical sources, Palestine does not have a Social Progress Snapshot.) Violent incidents and conflicts continue between Israel and Palestine in the territory, and Israel maintains a military presence there. Israel is a democracy surrounded by countries governed by Islamic rule. Lebanon, just north of Israel, has technically been at war with Israel since 1948.

The Near East remains a region of constant change and volatility, and these factors have led to its relatively lower ranking on the Social Progress Index.

The Arab Spring

In 2011 democratic uprisings occurred independently in several nations in the Arab world. They started in Tunisia and spread to Egypt, Libya, Syria, Yemen, Bahrain, Saudi Arabia, and Jordan. The term "Arab Spring" was used by Western media to describe this movement. The protests arose from long resentment over dictatorial governments, in addition to discontent over unemployment, harsh police tactics, corruption, and rising prices. While the protests did not knock down authoritarian regimes and replace them with democracies, many Arab governments made some reforms, such as increasing public representation in government, fighting corruption, improving salaries, and decreasing brutality by security forces. More than anything, the protests showed that the people in these countries wanted change.

Thousands gathered in the streets of Alexandria, Egypt, during the Arab Spring.

History

The Near East is the birthplace of three major religions—Judaism, Christianity, and Islam. Judaism is the oldest of the three. It began around 2000 BC with Abraham. He promoted the idea that there was one god (monotheism), called Yahweh or Jehovah, as opposed to the Romans, who believed in many gods (polytheism). Abraham had a grandson named Jacob, who was also called Israel. Descendants of Abraham became known as Israelites. According to Jewish sacred writings, or scriptures, the Israelites were enslaved in Egypt but led to freedom by Moses. Yahweh gave Moses the 10 Commandments, laws on right and wrong that form the basis of Judaism, at Mount Sinai. The Israelites went on to settle in what they called the Promised Land, or Canaan. Canaan included what today are Lebanon, Israel and Palestine, northwestern Jordan, and some western parts of Syria. Over time, Canaan was conquered by the Assyrians, the Babylonians, and eventually the Romans.

Christianity developed out of Judaism. Jesus of Nazareth was Jewish, and he preached to Jewish followers. His teachings became the basis of Christianity, which spread from Judea (present-day Israel), although Christians often worshiped in private early on because of persecution from the Romans. In the 4th century, however, Constantine took power as emperor of Rome. Under his rule, Christianity became the state religion, and by the end of the century it was illegal for any form of public worship other than Christianity in the entire Roman Empire.

According to tradition, Islam (which means "submission") began in 610, when the Prophet Muhammad had divine revelations delivered through an angel, which would become the Quran, the holy book of Islam, in Mecca, in what is now Saudi Arabia. Muhammad and his followers spread the teachings of Islam throughout the Arabian Peninsula. Over the next couple of hundred years, Islam became the predominant religion in the Near East and went on to be a popular religion in Africa and Asia as well. Muhammad believed in creating an Islamic state (or government) as well as a religious belief system. In Islam, there is no political/religious divide. Interestingly, many of the characters from Hebrew scripture appear in the Quran, including Abraham, Moses, David, Solomon, and the Queen of Sheba. A site called the Dome of the Rock in Jerusalem is revered by both Muslims and Jews. It is the location where Abraham prepared to sacrifice his son, Isaac (an important passage in the Torah, the first five books of Jewish scriptures). It is also the place where Muslims, followers of Islam, believe the Prophet Muhammad ascended into heaven.

The year 680 marked a split among followers of Islam—the two groups became the Shiites and the Sunni. The conflict between these two groups continues to be a source of turmoil in the Near East.

From the 8th to the 13th century, the Islamic world went through a period known as the Golden Age, when Arab Muslims were at the forefront of civilization and achievement. The Arab Empire covered Syria, Egypt, Persia (present-day Iran), North Africa, Palestine, Iraq, Armenia, Afghanistan, India, and Spain. Jerusalem also was controlled by the Arab Empire. Achievements made by Muslim communities during this time include the development of algebra, the magnetic compass, tools for navigation, the mastery of pens and printing, and a knowledge of how disease spreads and how it can be cured. During this period, Arabs were experts in numbers and computation theory. The capital of the Arab Empire at this time was in Baghdad in today's Iraq. A time of trade led to wealth and rich intellectual thought. Medicine, writing, mathematics, art, architecture, philosophy, banking, and business reached heights beyond the rest of the world.

For 600 years Islam was the most potent and vital religion, culture, and military force in the world. The successors and leaders after Muhammad were called caliphs, and the lands under their control were called caliphates.

In 1055 the Seljuk Turks conquered Baghdad. In 1099 Christian Crusaders took control of Baghdad. In the 1200s the Mongol tribes from the East swept through much of the Arab Empire, destroying cities, institutions, and the population in a brutal fashion. In 1260, however, Turkish ex-slaves in Egypt called the Malmuks would begin to drive back the Mongol invasion, even though

Portrait of Ottoman soldiers in Turkey.

Mongols would also in time embrace the Islamic religion. Over time Muslim rule would once again dominate the area, but under the Turks, not the Arabs.

In 1299 Osman I founded the Ottoman Empire, which was centered in the region of modern Turkey. Over the next 250 years, the Ottoman Empire would rise and expand, eventually defeating the Christian Byzantine Empire in 1453. The Byzantine Empire was the eastern half of the Roman Empire, centered in Constantinople, which is modern-day Istanbul, Turkey. While the western Roman Empire collapsed in 476, the Byzantine Empire lasted another 1,000 years. From the 16th to the early 20th century, most of the Arab world was under Ottoman rule. The Ottoman Empire included territories in Saudi Arabia, Yemen, Iran, Iraq, Kuwait, Israel, Lebanon, Syria, Jordan, Qatar, Bahrain, United Arab Emirates, and Palestine. The Ottoman rule also extended into Russia, Hungary, and all of North Africa.

The Ottomans sided with the Germans in World War I. When the war ended with the Ottomans on the losing side, the British controlled Syria, Palestine, and Mesopotamia (Iraq). In 1917, at the end of the war, Britain announced its intention to help establish a Jewish state in Palestine (the Balfour Declaration). Britain and France also agreed to divide the spoils of war—France would gain control of Syria and Lebanon, and Britain would take over Iraq, Jordan, and Palestine. Britain, largely through the assistance of Winston Churchill, who was then Britain's Secretary of State for the Colonies, carved out the country of Iraq, with little regard to the different groups living within newly established artificial borders.

The end of the Ottoman Empire led to the rise of Arab nationalism, which would make French and British control of the region difficult. Because of revolt among the Syrians, France signed a treaty with Syria in 1936 giving the country partial independence. Both Syria and Lebanon gained full independence after World War II. Lebanon formed a democratic government. The country is often considered the most diverse in the Near East. The Lebanese government is elected, but it works under a system called confessionalism, designed to provide some balance among the diverse groups there. Lebanon's president must come from the Christian community, the prime minister must be a Sunni Muslim, and the Speaker of the Parliament must be a Shia. This balance has helped maintain relative stability in the country. Also, the Muslim and Christian populations here tend to be more secular, or nonreligious, than in other countries. In general, the population breaks down as 54 percent Muslim with an almost even 27/27 percent split between Sunnis and Shia. About 40 percent are Christian, and the remainder are other religions.

Syria has gone through periods of military control, and while it does hold elections, their legitimacy is highly questionable, as the president maintains an authoritarian grip on the country. Lebanon holds elections, but they have been riddled with corruption. Britain ruled over Jordan until 1946 and Iraq until 1947. The next decades were characterized by a series of changes in leadership in Iraq. But the country became wealthy along the way by demanding a 50 percent tax on all oil profits. Saddam Hussein assumed the presidency in 1979 and ruled the country for 24 years. The United States backed Hussein when Iraq went to war against Iran (1980–1988), seeing Hussein's dictatorship as a means to maintain stability in the region and its connection to vast oil supplies.

Jordan battled over territory with Israel, but after signing a treaty in 1994, peace has been maintained between the two nations. Jordan today has a constitutional monarchy. Although there are some elected officials, the king maintains absolute control. Jordan has kept good relations with the United States and the West. As the situation in Syria has gotten worse, Jordan has accepted many thousands of refugees. In 2015 it hosted more than 628,000 Syrian refugees.

During World War I, Iran, which was known as Persia until 1935, remained neutral but wound up a battleground for Turkish, Russian, and British troops. In time the United States and the West worked to maintain the authoritarian control of the shah, who was basically the king of the country. In 1977 US President Jimmy Carter was toasting the Shah of Iran for maintaining an island of stability in a sea of turmoil. But two years later, the Iranian government would collapse as Islamic fundamentalists rose to power, overthrowing the shah. The new Iran

Portrait of the late Ayatollah
Khomeini, religious leader of Iran.

would be ruled by the religious leader the Ayatollah Ruhollah Khomeini. The country became a fierce enemy of the West, but it has gradually shifted away from this position. Still, Iran remains a country of contradictions—women enjoy full access to education, for example, but they are forbidden from watching men's sports in stadiums, and married women can't even leave the country without their husband's permission. While there are elections, the country is also governed by clergy. Authorities continue to disrupt the free flow of information.

The Kingdom of Saudi Arabia became an Islamic state on September 23, 1932, with Arabic as its national language and the Quran as its constitution. Saudi Arabia has long been controlled by a royal family, and the United States has had a long and fruitful relationship with the country, at least in terms of accessing oil. Oil has made Saudi Arabia one of the richest and most influential countries in the Near East. Oil also established Bahrain, the United Arab Emirates, Kuwait, and Oman as very prosperous nations in the Near East. Oman produces up to 980,000 barrels of oil a day, the UAE does 2 million, and Kuwait generates up to 2.5 million. While Bahrain may produce only up to 50,000 barrels a day, it provides oil-refining services. All of these countries have a strong ruler and ruling families. Oman operates like a monarchy. Kuwait has elections, but the al-Sabah family has been ruling over the region since 1756. The UAE is a federation of seven hereditary absolute monarchies. The rulers of each emirate are called emirs.

The one country surrounded by these oil-rich countries that has fared the worst is Yemen. Yemen's government has been marred by civil war, economic mismanagement, and corruption, and it is the poorest nation in the Near East. Without strong leadership, there has been unrest between warring factions in the country. Two-thirds of the population are Shiite, while one-third is Sunni.

A Word About the Kurds

The Kurds, who are mostly Sunni Muslim, are a non-Arab ethnic group that has long strived to establish its own nation in the Near East. They are united by a Kurdish language and culture. Historically, the Kurds have lived in areas around the Zagros Mountains in territories that are part of Iraq, Syria, Iran, Turkey, and Armenia. They have long desired to establish their own nation of Kurdistan—the closest region resembling this is Iraqi Kurdistan, a semi-autonomous area in northern Iraq. Some historians say that the British missed an opportunity to establish Kurdistan after World War I and the fall of the Ottoman Empire. The Kurds have often been in conflict with the nations where they live. They have often been persecuted as countries such as Turkey have seen them as a threat, pushing for sovereignty. Today, Kurds are in the spotlight, as they have been on the frontlines in the fight against the terrorist group ISIS.

Kurdish officers partake in training to fight ISIS. After completing the training program, they will pass their knowledge to others in Iraq.

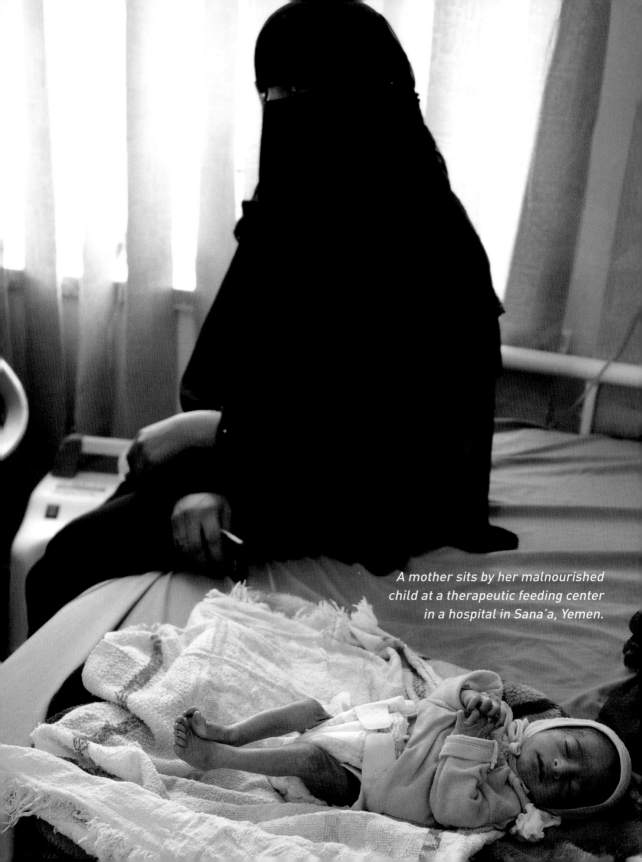

A mother sits by her malnourished child at a therapeutic feeding center in a hospital in Sana'a, Yemen.

CHAPTER 1

BASIC HUMAN NEEDS

Words to Understand

Aquifer: an underground layer of water-bearing rock, from which groundwater can be extracted using a water well.

Ecosystem: the interaction between all living things—plants, animals, and microscopic organisms—in a particular place or area and their environment, which includes the air, water, and soil.

Groundwater: water that is stored naturally underground.

Seawater intrusion: the movement of seawater, or salt water, into fresh water sources, such as aquifers.

Undernourishment: not getting enough food or good-quality food to promote health or proper growth.

In general, the foods that are staples of the Near East are very healthy. Meals often feature dates, figs, wheat, barley, rice, and meat. In coastal regions, people eat fish. Yogurt, nuts, lentils, chick peas, olive oil, lemons, spinach, pomegranates, parsley, mint, cucumbers, and eggplant are all widely consumed. Regional spices such as sesame, cumin, turmeric, and cinnamon are all very healthy. Overall in the region, **undernourishment** is low—less than 5 percent of people there are undernourished, according to the World Family Map 2015 (childtrends.org).

Still, while the foods common to the region can provide the foundation for sound nutrition, many people here are not getting enough. Undernourishment may be worst in Yemen, where about 30 percent of the population has been consistently undernourished and poverty levels are high, according to the World Bank. Iraq, which has weathered war and much civil strife, has seen undernourishment rise from 10 percent of its population in 1991 to more than 26 percent in 2012. In Palestine the undernourished population has grown from 14.7 percent to almost 32 percent in that same period.

The civil war in Syria has only worsened malnutrition in that country. The nonprofit organization Save the Children (savethechildren.org) estimates that

Qatar's cutting-edge health care is on display for Princess Lalla Salma of Morocco as she attends the World Innovation Summit for Health, in Doha, Qatar.

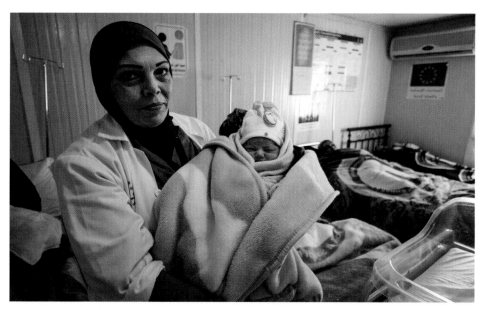

A doctor holds a baby in the maternity center at the Zaatari refugee camp in Jordan, which hosts around 80,000 Syrians.

more than 2 million children are at risk of malnutrition there. Those caught in the conflict have been unable to produce or buy enough food, while prices have soared and the food production industry has collapsed. The United Nations

Jordan: A Medical Tourism Destination

Because Jordan has been praised for its high-quality medical care at reasonable prices, it has attracted patients from around the world. Tens of thousands of people have come from nearby Iraq and Palestine alone. Treatment costs can be 25 percent less than in the United States. People travel here for cancer treatment, cosmetic surgery, cardiovascular work, infertility treatment, and more. Dubai (one of the United Arab Emirates) and Lebanon also provide superior health treatment at a comparatively low price.

program UNICEF (unicef.org) has said that the refugees fleeing the war-torn nation have also faced a dangerous lack of food.

On the positive side, Saudi Arabia, Lebanon, Israel, Iran, Jordan, and Kuwait score above 96 on the SPI for meeting Nutrition and Basic Medical Care. Again, health care suffers most in areas where there has been civil unrest. In the fall of 2015, *Middle East Health* magazine reported that a quarter of all health facilities in Yemen were no longer operating fully. On the other hand, countries like Bahrain and Qatar have established state-of-the-art medical facilities. Health care workers who treat those who are opposed to the established governments, however, may be punished or risk their lives. In Bahrain doctors and nurses who treated wounded protesters in the 2011 uprising were arrested, and some were tortured.

A Water Shortage

Much of the Near East is characterized by dry desert lands with water more scarce here than in other parts of the world. Millions of people lack access to safe, reliable water, according to the Water Project (thewaterproject.org). The overuse of water in agriculture is affecting the countries' already stressed water resources. The cost of water in Jordan has increased 30 percent in 10 years due to a shortage of groundwater. Iran has warned its people of insufficient water supplies. Iran's Lake Urmia, the Near East's largest lake, has lost 95 percent of its water since 1996. The UN has labeled water Iran's "most important human security challenge." In the Palestinian territory of Gaza, seawater intrusion and the leakage of sewage have made 95 percent

Satellite images of Lake Urmia drying up between 2000 and 2015.

of the coastal aquifer undrinkable. Villages and farms in Syria and Iraq have been abandoned as water sources have run dry. Even rich countries like the United Arab Emirates are facing a serious loss of available water resources. Lack of water has led to more malnutrition because not enough crops can be grown for food.

To solve the water crisis, Saudi Arabia, Kuwait, Bahrain, and the UAE have turned increasingly to desalination plants that change seawater to fresh water, but the process is expensive. Also, excess salt has been returned to the oceans in the Persian Gulf, threatening the ecosystem there. Jordan has established programs to license and train operators, managers, and engineers in water and wastewater treatment. Many in the region encourage the use of low-flow faucets, low-flow showerheads, low-flush and composting toilets, and water-saving dishwashers and clothes washers to help conserve this precious resource.

Lebanon Rubbish Crisis

From the middle of summer 2015 into the fall of that year, rubbish piled up in Lebanon's capital city of Beirut, creating an environmental emergency and slowing down commerce in the region. A group of citizens started a movement called You Stink, demanding a solution to the trash buildup but also pointing out the corruption and ineffectiveness in government. Nearby landfills have reached overcapacity, and activists blame politicians who had been warned about the problem but failed to reach agreements with waste-removal businesses. Proper waste management is key to a nation's health and a factor in determining a nation's position on the Social Progress Index.

A man sifts through a large garbage pile in Beirut, Lebanon.

The Qat Problem in Yemen

In addition to dealing with great civil unrest and poverty in Yemen, citizens here cope with a continuing drug addiction crisis. The majority of Yemenis chew a green leaf called qat (or khat), which is a mild narcotic, or stimulant. It's estimated that as much as 90 percent of Yemeni men use qat, and one in four women chew it. Some see it as the equivalent of alcohol in the West, since Islam forbids drinking alcohol. Pro-qat users say it provides a mild euphoria or sense of excitement. Critics have said that qat makes people more lazy, and can lead to mental illness, as well as tooth loss and heart disease. The plant controls appetite and may be increasing levels of malnourishment. Qat can be easy to cultivate, and farmers can earn more money raising it than growing food. The crop has been draining Yemen's water supply, and experts have said that stopping qat production would greatly increase the amount of household water available.

A man chews and sells the popular narcotic qat at a local market.

Safe and Sound at Home

Access to shelter and electricity is a relative weakness throughout the Near East, even in rich countries such as Saudi Arabia and Kuwait. An article in the Middle East Online (middle-east-online.com) found that there was a shortage of 3.5 million homes in the region. "While there is currently an oversupply of upscale or luxury housing in many markets, there remains a shortage of . . . affordable dwellings across the major markets" in the area, said international property agent Jones Lang LaSalle in a November 2011 study. Some real estate developers in Dubai and Saudi Arabia have made pledges to create more lower-income and middle-income housing. Dubai, which has been a land of luxury, has seen a surge in affordable housing.

Negev Desert, one of the sunniest places in Israel, is the prime location for the solar industry. Benefiting from the solar panels, Israel is close to supplying 100 percent of its population with electricity.

According to the World Bank, many countries in the Near East have close to 100 percent access to electricity—these nations include Iran, Iraq, Qatar, Oman, Lebanon, Saudi Arabia, and Israel. Even war-torn Syria has reported that 96 percent of its population has a connection to power. Yemen, however, falls to the bottom, with just 48 percent having electricity.

It may not be a surprise that the Near East is not the safest place in the world to live. What may be a surprise is the fact that more deaths are caused by traffic accidents than from wars and conflicts. The World Health

Yemeni teenagers pose with a Kalashnikov rifle in the Hadhramaut Valley, Yemen.

Organization has said that the number of road accident deaths is more than double the number in the United States. Saudi Arabia, in particular, has one of the highest traffic death rates. An average of 17 Saudi Arabian residents die on the country's roads each day. Saudi analysts have said that the country lacks any sort of driver education and respect for driving rules. Running red lights and illegal U-turns are common. In Iran traffic accidents represent a high number of the country's fatalities.

Still, safety from violent crime is a problem in many regions. In this SPI category, Iraq scores 21.9, Syria 31.24, Yemen 48.8, and Iran 53.14. Finding a sense of security and safety is very difficult in these countries, and it has led to a massive movement of people from these lands. Millions have journeyed to Europe and elsewhere trying to find better lives.

Text-Dependent Questions

1. What is the primary source of wealth in the Near East?
2. What resource is in short supply in the Near East?
3. What is one solution to declining fresh water supplies?
4. What is a surprising cause of many deaths in the Near East—greater than death by gun violence?
5. Which country is poorest in the region?

Research Project

In the Near East, water supplies are running low in many areas. California is facing low supplies of water as well. Write down 10 ways people might be able to conserve water. For example, a large percent of water is wasted in the laundry room—always do a full load to conserve.

The nonprofit organization the Water Project says the Near East faces a critical water shortage. There are many approaches to water conservation, however, that countries could be using, such as limiting landscape watering, reusing air conditioning condensation, and using more efficient irrigation techniques in agriculture. Many sources on the Internet provide information on how countries can conserve on water use. Write seven ways that the Near East might be able to use less water.

Children of Iraqi host community and Syrian Kurdish refugees attending school in the Duhok area in the Kurdish Region of Iraq. The schools are located in the poorer areas in Duhok near refugee camps and receive support from international aid organizations.

CHAPTER 2

FOUNDATIONS OF WELL-BEING

Words to Understand

Greenhouse gas emissions: the release into the earth's atmosphere of gases, especially carbon dioxide, that absorb infrared radiation from the sun, which heats the air. The more of these gases that exist, the more heat is prevented from escaping into space and, consequently, the more the earth's atmosphere gets warmer. This increase in heat is known as the "greenhouse effect."

Life expectancy: the average number of years that a person may expect to live.

Pollutants: substances, especially chemicals or waste products, that make the air, soil, or water unsafe.

Primary education: generally, basic education for children (usually ages 5 to 11), including reading, writing, and basic math. For most countries, primary education is mandatory. Also called elementary education.

Sect: a religious group that is a smaller part of a larger group and whose members all share similar beliefs.

According to UNICEF, access to quality education is not a privilege but a basic human right. Generally, countries in the Near East have made great improvements in providing basic education for their young people over the past 25 years. In 2005 UNICEF praised Bahrain, Jordan, Lebanon, Palestine, Qatar, and Syria for pushing close to universal standards for primary school. Quality of education, school dropout rates, and the gender gap in the number of girls and boys in school, however, remain problems in the region. Yemen again ranks lowest when it comes to education.

The website Children and Youth in History (chnm.gmu.edu) has found that access to **primary education** has improved dramatically in the Near East, but the public schools suffer from overcrowded classes led by poorly trained teachers with inadequate materials. The curriculum is for the most part secular, or nonreligious. Islamic religious schools known as madrasas are common throughout the Near East. Curriculum in madrasas is centered on the Quran. Between 2000 and 2010, enrollment in secondary schools increased by just over 10 percent in the Middle East and North Africa region, according to the World Bank.

The foundations for basic education in the Near East are generally weaker than in Europe and the United States, but some spots are brighter than others. The World Bank says that the region has made great improvements in education. It has quadrupled the average level of schooling since 1960, halved illiteracy since 1980, and achieved almost complete gender equality for primary education. In Iran, for example, the literacy rate for children is 98.7 percent and 85 percent for adults, according to the World Bank. The total literacy rate is highest in Israel (98 percent), followed by Jordan (95 percent), Saudi Arabia (94.7 percent), Lebanon (about 94 percent), Oman (91 percent), and Iraq (almost 80 percent), but just 70 percent in Yemen.

Public education in Saudi Arabia—from primary schools to high schools—is available to everyone and is free. Islamic religious studies are featured.

Syrian schoolchildren head to their schools on the first day of the new school year in Damascus, capital of Syria. Syria's Education Ministry said a total of 4 million students attended 15,000 schools nationwide on the first day of the new school year.

Schooling covers 6 years of primary education, 3 years of intermediate (junior high school in the US), and 3 years of secondary (high school). The Saudi government has also established more than 150 vocational schools in an effort to create more than three million jobs in 10 years in areas other than oil production and processing.

School attendance in Israel is mandatory from ages 6 to 18. In Israel the majority of students attend state schools, but there are state schools that emphasize Jewish studies, as well as Arab and Druze schools that focus on Arabic and Druze religions, history, and culture. (The Druze religion is an Arabic sect of Islam.)

Some of the Israeli secondary schools offer specialized education to train technicians, engineers, agriculture experts, and military personnel. There are also yeshiva schools, which concentrate on Jewish studies. The World Bank says that enrollment of males and females in primary and secondary school is about equal in number.

The Education for All Global Monitoring Report published by UNESCO, an agency of the United Nations that supports educational, scientific, and cultural improvements and exchanges, found that many children in Arab states leave school with a lack of skills needed for the workplace—10.5 million young people ages 15 to 24 years never complete primary school in this region. The organization stressed, however, that Jordan is an exception. Jordan is a success story in education, as primary school enrollment increased from 71 percent in1994 to 98.2 percent in 2006.

Cell Phone and Internet Use

A Gallup poll found that 83 percent of people in the UAE have both cell phone and home Internet access. More than 94 percent of the population in Bahrain, Jordan, Qatar, Israel, Kuwait, and Saudi Arabia have a cell phone. About 8 in 10 have a cell phone in Lebanon. The numbers are 88 percent in Iraq, 64 percent

Visitors to an Internet cafe in Tehran, Iran, surf the Web.

in Iran and Syria, and 55 percent in Yemen. Internet access at home is far less. While it's 84 percent in the UAE, it's 77 percent in Israel, 73 percent in Kuwait, 59 percent in Saudi Arabia, 34 percent in Iran, 23 percent in Syria, 12 percent in Jordan, and just 3 percent in Yemen.

Many citizens in Bahrain have been seeking political reforms that go against the monarchy there. Bahrain has slowly strangled the country's Internet connection, fearing that news of unrest coming in or out of the country would only lead to more protests.

Health and Wellness

In 2013 the World Bank looked at health issues that were mostly associated with developed nations and found that people living in the Near East were at increased risk. Some of the leading causes of premature death in this region are heart disease (up 44 percent since 1990), stroke (up 35 percent), and diabetes (up 87 percent).

Overall, countries in the Near East get low scores when it comes to health and wellness. For a benchmark, consider that life expectancy in the United States is almost 79 years, according to World Bank 2012 statistics. In Norway and the UK, it's 81. In the Near East, Yemen hits a low, with 63 years. Compare that to 82 in Israel, almost 80 in Lebanon, 76 in Bahrain and Oman, and 75 in Saudi Arabia. Surprisingly, the people of Syria may live to an average of 74 years and to 69 in Iraq, but perhaps these numbers do not take into account the recent turmoil from ISIS, civil war, and random acts of terrorism that disrupt life in these countries.

While some areas of the Near East suffer from insufficient food, other regions are facing more modern-day health problems such as obesity and diabetes. In 2015 the cable news channel CNN reported that obesity and diabetes rates in the Near East are staggering, particularly in the Gulf region—Kuwait, Saudi Arabia, Bahrain, Qatar, and the United Arab Emirates. In many of these countries where there is wealth, people often are not very active, living in air-conditioned environments and working jobs where they sit in front of computers all day. About 37 million people are living with diabetes in the Near East and North Africa, according to the International Diabetes

To encourage healthful behavior, the UAE has built bike paths—such as this—next to residential communities. It includes a walkway, jogging track, benches, retail kiosks, and toilets.

Federation. Recently, these countries have started to take measures to counteract "lifestyle" diseases like diabetes and cardiovascular disease. The UAE, for example, has set up bike paths and promoted physical activities such as volleyball and water sports.

One unexpected positive outcome of the conflicts in the Near East has been a decrease in air pollution. A report in *Science Advances* showed that political and social upheaval in Syria, Iraq, and Palestine, for example, has led to a downturn in economic development and industry, which resulted in much lower amounts of **pollutants**. Overall deaths attributed to air pollution are lower in the Near East than in the United States or Germany. In several countries in the Near East, **greenhouse gas emissions** are lower than in the United States, but not by much. Greenhouse gas emissions include carbon dioxide, methane, nitrous oxide, sulphur hexafluoride, hydrofluorocarbons, and perfluorocarbons. They are often measured together as "carbon dioxide equivalents." The GDP, or gross domestic product, takes into account production and consumption levels—it's used in measuring greenhouse gas levels. While the United States has about a 421 of carbon dioxide equivalents per GDP, the UAE has 419, Saudi Arabia has 390, Jordan, 357, Israel 371, and Yemen 309. Some Near Eastern countries are higher: Iraq (546) and Iran (594). Kuwait has a whopping 759, and Oman has a 737. Most of the countries have made little effort to maintain biodiversity, but Saudi Arabia has made a commitment to the conservation of biodiversity and the protection of wildlife.

The suicide rate in the Near East is much lower than in other parts of the world, and Islam's strong condemnation of suicide probably plays a role. Saudi Arabia, in fact, has the lowest suicide rate on the planet, according to the SPI. Studies have shown that severe depression and anxiety are common in this region, most likely due to the continuing conflicts there, but still suicide rates are not high.

Text-Dependent Questions

1. What country has the highest literacy rate in the Near East?
2. What is Druze?
3. What is one unexpected positive of conflicts in the Near East?
4. What are some of the modern-day health problems seen in the Near East?

Research Project

Choose a country in the Near East and research its education system. How does the school system in that country compare to your own? What are the similarities, and what are the differences? If you'd like to take it an extra step, try finding a student pen pal in the Near East and get his or her personal story about the school experience. The website Students of the World (studentsoftheworld.info/penpals) can help you to find a pen pal.

انتخابات المجلس البلدي لمدينة الرياض

الدائرة الانتخابية الرابعة (الدورة الثالثة)

المركز الانتخابي رقم (١١٧١) (نساء)

Saudi women stand outside a polling station after casting their votes in the kingdom's municipal elections, in Riyadh, Saudi Arabia. For the first time Saudi women have been allowed to run and vote in the country's municipal elections, regarded as a small but significant opening of the ultra-conservative society to women. Female candidates, however, were not allowed to campaign, and women had to be accompanied by male guardians in order to be able to vote.

CHAPTER 3

OPPORTUNITY

In the category of Opportunity, the Near East does not score very high compared to North America, Europe, South America, and other regions. When Freedom House (freedomhouse.org) evaluated the region, the Near East as a whole scored only 5 percent free, with the press only 2 percent free. Censorship is common. Israel fares better than other countries in the region and is the only one with a free press. Lebanon and Kuwait are considered partly free.

Jordan also has more freedom compared to other countries in the Near East. However, it criminalizes speech that is critical of the king, government officials and institutions, and Islam, as well as speech considered defamatory to other persons. Jordan is a constitutional monarchy with

After a firefight in the Gaza Strip, several buildings were destroyed.

some government-appointed officials and some elected representatives. The king maintains near total control over Jordanian politics, signing and executing all laws. He can dissolve parliament whenever he wishes, and he controls the military.

Although Israel is considered free, it has committed human rights violations in its treatment of Palestinians, according to Amnesty International. In 2014 a 50-day military offensive in the Gaza Strip killed over 1,500 Palestinian civilians, including 539 children, and wounded thousands more civilians. The area is ruled by Hamas, an anti-Israeli terrorist group, which has carried out

Women's Rights

In the 1950s Iraq became the first Arab nation to have a female government minister and to have a law that gave women the right to divorce. Women gained the right to vote and run for public office in 1980. But under the current government, women have less of a role in the workplace. Under Saddam Hussein, women were actually more part of the workforce in marketing, farming, and professional services. Violence against women and a lack of legal protection are on the rise in Iraq. Saudi Arabia, Syria, and Kuwait also allow women to vote and run for office. In some Arab countries, women need permission from a male in the family to travel. Jordan is one exception. Here women hold jobs as pilots, police officers, and soldiers. Still, in Saudi Arabia, women may be punished for not wearing required clothing. They cannot even drive without a male relative in the car. In Syria the government has used torture and violence against women as a tool of war. Women in Israel and Lebanon have many more freedoms—moving about freely and dressing as they wish. Israeli women have the right to vote, freedom of speech, and equal access to education and the workplace. Lebanese women enjoy almost equal civil rights as men. Iran, which has often been criticized by the West, actually has fairly strong support for women's rights, especially when it comes to education. The country's education system is producing highly skilled female doctors, business owners, and teachers.

Three women, dressed in their hijab, walk through the market among men.

thousands of rocket and mortar attacks on Israel. In Israel about 19 percent of the population are non-Jews (815,000 Muslims, 163,000 Christians, and 96,000 Druze). All have equal voting rights, including women. Arabs have held government posts, and 200,000 Arabs attend Israeli schools. The law here maintains rights for religious freedom, to peacefully change the government, to join and establish labor organizations, and to own land. The country has broad antidiscrimination laws to prevent discrimination on the basis of sex, marital status, or sexual orientation.

Saudi Arabia ranks low on the SPI when it comes to personal rights. Human Rights Watch (hrw.org) says that the country continues to try, convict, and imprison political dissidents and human rights activists solely because of their peaceful activities. For example, Reif Badawi, a blogger accused of insulting Islam, was sentenced to **flogging** and 10 years in prison. Discrimination against women and religious minorities is common. Saudi Arabia does not tolerate public worship by believers of religions other than Islam. The Ministry of Justice has filed cases against sorcery, or witchcraft, which can be punishable by death. Migrant workers are often exploited.

Although Iran elected a moderate candidate, Hassan Rouhani, to be president in 2013, the country has seen no significant improvements in human rights. Repressive elements within the security and intelligence forces and the judiciary retain wider powers and continue to be accused of human rights abuses. In 2014 Iran had the second highest number of executions in the world after China and executed the largest number of juvenile offenders. The country remains one of the biggest jailers in the world of journalists, bloggers, and social media activists.

Iranian President Hassan Rouhani prepares for a press conference in Tehran.

Human Rights Watch says that personal rights in Iraq and Syria have crumbled as rebel groups and government forces intensified their fight against each other and ISIS. The fighting has forced millions from their homes in both countries.

Tolerance

Historically, the Near East was a place for religious **tolerance** for many centuries. From the 700s to the 1200s, the Arab world followed an Islamic belief that called for protection of "People of the Book," or Jews and Christians. The Ottoman Empire from the 16th to 20th century also stressed religious tolerance. The Social Progress Imperative gives poor marks overall to the Near East when it comes to tolerance today.

For centuries, Jews lived and thrived in Babylon, located in modern-day Iraq. The Jewish community in Baghdad numbered about 140,000 in 1940 but has dropped to practically zero today. In 2011 WikiLeaks claimed there were just seven Jews living there. The Christian population in Iraq was at more than one million in 2003 and was estimated at less than 300,000 by 2014. The World Values Survey in 2013 named Jordan one of the least tolerant countries in the world—51.4 percent of the population there said they would refuse to live next to someone of a different race. The Near East deals with large numbers of low-skilled immigrants from South Asia, and that seems to have created a hotbed of racial tension.

Gallup polls have found the Lebanese to be fairly tolerant. In one of the Gallup surveys in Lebanon, more than three-quarters of respondents strongly agreed with this statement: "I would not object to a person of a different religious faith moving next door." That number is higher than in Belgium (65 percent), the UK (57 percent), Germany (57 percent), Italy (53 percent), and Israel (23 percent).

Gay Rights

The Near East as a whole is very conservative, and homosexuality is often regarded as a crime. Iran, Saudi Arabia, and Yemen have laws that may subject a person engaging in same-sex behavior to flogging or death. A man found to be gay in Syria may be sentenced to five years of hard labor. Lebanon may be the most tolerant in the region. Lebanon has gay bars and nightclubs as well as the first association for gay people in the Near East, called the Helem Foundation. It was founded in 2004 with a mission to promote gay rights in Lebanon and to help the Ministry of Health support AIDS awareness in the country. Lesbian, gay, bisexual,

Although the LGBT community is widely accepted in several countries, there are still plenty who suffer torture, or even the death penalty, for who they are. Here, a young woman protests in Sweden for the gay community of Iran, seeking justice for those who have lost their lives.

and transgender (LGBT) rights in Israel are very advanced. Israel allows Jews to immigrate to Israel with their non-Jewish same-sex spouses and has allowed gay pride parades. Couples in Israel can receive recognition of their partner relationship and of many rights connected to it. Tolerance of homosexuality may be rising in some unexpected places. An article in *The Muslim Observer* said that in Kuwait and Saudi Arabia, more homosexuals are congregating in public, and while not broadcasting their sexuality, they are not hiding it either.

Higher Education

Israel far exceeds the other countries in the region in the category of Access to Advanced Education. Many citizens in the Near East do not go on to earn a college degree, but in some sectors where there is a growing middle class, more students are heading to college. The United Arab Emirates, Palestine, and Kuwait have been reporting higher enrollment rates for women than for men. There are international college campuses in the UAE, Qatar, Bahrain, and Saudi Arabia.

Qatar's Education City strives to encourage students to achieve their dreams.

Text-Dependent Questions

1. True or false: Many countries in the Near East tolerate speech that is critical of the ruling government.
2. Was there a time when the Arab world was more tolerant of different religions and ethnic backgrounds?
3. Which two countries seem to offer the most personal rights in the Near East?
4. Which country was named one of the least tolerant in a poll?
5. Which country has the most number of executions in the world after China?

Research Project

The press is often censored in the Near East. Can you find examples of censorship in US history? The Near East also curbs many personal rights. What are some examples of personal rights that have been suppressed in the United States? You might start by checking the Amnesty International web site (http://www.amnestyusa.org/our-work/countries/americas/usa). Amnesty International works to protect human rights around the world. The organization advocates for human rights–oriented approaches to national security, criminal justice and police accountability; works to abolish the death penalty; and campaigns for individuals at risk.

Visitors take photos of the skyline of Abu Dhabi, the capital of the United Arab Emirates.

CHAPTER 4

NEAR EAST COUNTRIES AT A GLANCE

BAHRAIN

QUICK STATS

Population: 1,346,613
Urban Population: 88.8% of total population (2015)
Comparative Size: 3.5 times the size of Washington, DC
Gross Domestic Product (per capita): $51,700 (2014 est.)
Gross Domestic Product (by sector): agriculture 0.3%, industry 47.1%, services 52.6% (2014 est.)
Government: constitutional monarchy
Languages: Arabic (official), English, Farsi, Urdu

SOCIAL PROGRESS SNAPSHOT

Foundations of Well-being: 67.17 (+0.72 above/below 66.45 world average)
Opportunity: 46.94 (–1.29 above/below 48.23 world average)
(Not all scores computed due to data gaps in statistical sources.)

In 1783 the Sunni Al-Khalifa family took power in Bahrain, and it became a British protectorate in the 1800s. The country gained independence in 1971. Facing declining oil reserves, Bahrain has turned to petroleum processing and refining and international banking. Bahrain's small size requires it to play a delicate balancing act in foreign affairs among its larger neighbors. The Sunni-led government has struggled to manage relations with its large Shia-majority population. In early 2011, amid Arab uprisings elsewhere in the region, the Bahraini government confronted similar protests. Ongoing dissatisfaction has led to sporadic clashes between demonstrators and security forces.

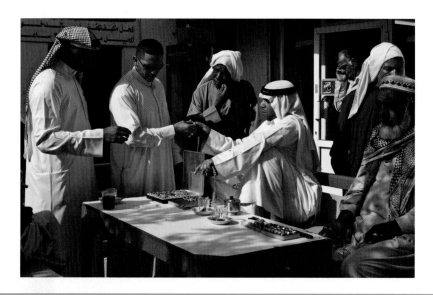

Locals bargain for the purchase of an item at the market in Manama, Bahrain.

Follow the index every year at socialprogressimperative.org.
Quick Stats from CIA World Factbook.

NEAR EAST COUNTRIES AT A GLANCE   **61**

Iranians drink tea during the Shi'ite Tasua, a day ahead of the Ashura religious festival in Tehran's Grand Bazaar.

IRAN

QUICK STATS

Population: 81,824,270 (2015 est.)
Urban Population: 73.4% of total population (2015)
Comparative Size: almost 2.5 times the size of Texas; slightly smaller than Alaska
Gross Domestic Product (per capita): $17,100 (2014 est.)
Gross Domestic Product (by sector): agriculture 9.1%, industry 40.7%, services 50.3% (2014 est.)
Government: theocratic republic
Languages: Persian (official), Azeri Turkic and Turkic dialects, Kurdish, Gilaki and Mazandarani, Luri, Balochi, Arabic, other

SOCIAL PROGRESS SNAPSHOT

Social Progress Index: 56.82 (–4.18 above/below 61 world average)
Basic Human Needs: 78.42 (+10.09 above/below 68.33 world average)
Foundations of Well-being: 61.14 (–5.31 above/below 66.45 world average)
Opportunity: 30.90 (–17.33 above/below 48.23 world average)

Known as Persia until 1935, Iran became an Islamic republic in 1979 after the ruling monarchy was overthrown. Conservative clerical forces led by the Ayatollah Ruhollah Khomeini established a theocratic, or religion-based, system of government with a religious scholar (the Supreme Leader) having ultimate political authority. In June 2009 nationwide protests were held over allegations of electoral fraud. In June 2013 Iranians elected a moderate conservative cleric, Dr. Hassan Rouhani, as president. A recent deal between Iran and an international coalition, led by the US, UK, France, Russia, China, and Germany, over Iran's development of nuclear power and weapons has led to the lifting of sanctions against it.

IRAQ

QUICK STATS

Population: 37,056,169 (July 2015 est.)
Urban Population: 69.5% of total population (2015)
Comparative Size: slightly more than three times the size of New York state
Gross Domestic Product (per capita): $14,600 (2014 est.)
Gross Domestic Product (by sector): agriculture: 3.3%, industry: 64.5%, services: 32.2% (2014 est.)
Government: parliamentary democracy
Languages: Arabic (official), Kurdish (official), Turkmen (a Turkish dialect) and Assyrian (Neo-Aramaic) are official in areas where they constitute a majority of the population, Armenian

SOCIAL PROGRESS SNAPSHOT

Social Progress Index: 48.35 (–12.65 above/below 61 world average)
Basic Human Needs: 63.11 (–5.22 above/below 68.33 world average)
Foundations of Well-being: 55.29 (–11.16 above/below 66.45 world average)
Opportunity: 26.67 (–21.56 above/below 48.23 world average)

Formerly part of the Ottoman Empire, Iraq was occupied by Britain during World War I. It attained its independence as a kingdom in 1932. A republic was proclaimed in 1958, but strongmen ruled the country until 2003. Iraq fought a costly eight-year war (1980–1988) with Iran. After a US-led UN coalition defeated Iraq's attack on Kuwait, the UN Security Council required Iraq to scrap all weapons of mass destruction and long-range missiles. A US-led invasion of Iraq in March 2003 ousted President Saddam Hussein. A civil war followed the invasion, and US forces remained in Iraq until 2011. Iraq transitioned to a constitutional government. Since early 2015, Iraq has fought ISIS to recapture lost territory.

ISRAEL

QUICK STATS

Population: 8,049,314 (includes populations of the Golan Heights of Golan Sub-District and East Jerusalem, which was annexed by Israel after 1967) (2014 est.)
Urban Population: 92.1% of total population (2015)
Comparative Size: slightly larger than New Jersey
Gross Domestic Product (per capita): $32,700 (2014 est.)
Gross Domestic Product (by sector): agriculture 2.4%, industry 25.7%, services 71.9% (2014 est.)
Government: parliamentary democracy
Languages: Hebrew (official), Arabic (used officially for Arab minority), English (most commonly used foreign language)

SOCIAL PROGRESS SNAPSHOT

Social Progress Index: 72.60 (+11.60 above/below 61 world average)
Basic Human Needs: 86.96 (+18.63 above/below 68.33 world average)
Foundations of Well-being: 72.99 (+6.54 above/below 66.45 world average)
Opportunity: 57.85 (+9.62 above/below 48.23 world average)

An Israeli state was declared in 1948, and the Israelis subsequently defeated the Arabs in a series of wars. In 1982 Israel withdrew from the Sinai following the 1979 Israel-Egypt Peace Treaty. In 1993 Israeli and Palestinian officials signed a Declaration of Principles (also known as the Oslo Accords), supporting the idea of a two-state solution and an interim period of Palestinian self-rule. Outstanding disputes with Jordan were resolved in 1994. Progress toward a permanent status agreement with the Palestinians was undermined by Israeli-Palestinian violence between 2001 and February 2005. Israel in 2005 unilaterally disengaged from the Gaza Strip, evacuating settlers and its military while retaining control over most points of entry. The election of the anti-Israeli group Hamas to head the Palestinian Legislative Council in 2006 froze relations between Israel and the Palestinian Authority and has led to a series of conflicts. Palestine, which includes the West Bank, the Gaza Strip, and East Jerusalem, was recognized as a nonmember observer state by the United Nations in 2012. Violent incidents and conflicts continue between Israel and Palestine in the territory, and Israel maintains a military presence there.

JORDAN

QUICK STATS

Population: 8,117,564
Urban Population: 83.7% of total population (2015)
Comparative Size: about three-quarters the size of Pennsylvania; slightly smaller than Indiana
Gross Domestic Product (per capita): $11,900 (2014 est.)
Gross Domestic Product (by sector): agriculture 3.2%, industry 29.3%, services 67.4% (2014 est.)
Government: constitutional monarchy
Languages: Arabic (official), English (widely understood among upper and middle classes)

SOCIAL PROGRESS SNAPSHOT

Social Progress Index: 63.31 (+2.31 above/below 61 world average)
Basic Human Needs: 82.63 (+14.30 above/below 68.33 world average)
Foundations of Well-being: 64.93 (-1.52 above/below 66.45 world average)
Opportunity: 42.38 (-5.85 above/below 48.23 world average)

Following World War I and the breakup of the Ottoman Empire, Britain governed much of the Middle East. Britain demarcated a region called Transjordan from Palestine in the early 1920s. The area gained its independence in 1946, becoming the Kingdom of Jordan. King Hussein successfully navigated competing pressures from the major powers (the US, Soviet Union, and UK), various Arab states, Israel, and a large internal Palestinian population. Jordan lost the West Bank to Israel in the 1967 Six-Day War. In 1994 Hussein signed a peace treaty with Israel. Following Hussein's death in 1999, his eldest son, King Abdullah II, assumed the throne. He implemented modest political and economic reforms, but Jordanians continue to press for further reforms.

KUWAIT

QUICK STATS

Population: 2,788,534
Urban Population: 98.3% of total population (2015)
Comparative Size: slightly smaller than New Jersey
Gross Domestic Product (per capita): $71,000 (2014 est.)
Gross Domestic Product (by sector): agriculture 0.3%, industry 49.4%, services 50.2% (2014 est.)
Government: constitutional emirate
Languages: Arabic (official), English widely spoken

SOCIAL PROGRESS SNAPSHOT

Social Progress Index: 69.19 (+8.19 above/below 61 world average)
Basic Human Needs: 86.28 (+17.95 above/below 68.33 world average)
Foundations of Well-being: 73.96 (+7.51 above/below 66.45 world average)
Opportunity: 47.35 (-0.88 above/below 48.23 world average)

Britain oversaw foreign relations and defense for the ruling Kuwaiti Al-Sabah dynasty from 1899 until independence in 1961. Kuwait was attacked by Iraq in1990, but a US-led UN coalition liberated Kuwait in four days. The Al-Sabah family has ruled since returning to power in 1991 and reestablished an elected legislature that has become increasingly assertive. Four women were elected to its National Assembly. Demonstrators forced the prime minister to resign in late 2011. In late 2012, Kuwait witnessed unprecedented protests in response to changes to the electoral law. Since 2006 the emir has dissolved the National Assembly five times and shuffled the cabinet, usually citing political gridlock.

Local residents buy food in Beirut.

LEBANON

QUICK STATS

Population: 6,184,701 (2015 est.)
Urban Population: 87.8% of total population (2015)
Comparative Size: about one-third the size of Maryland
Gross Domestic Product (per capita): $18,000 (2014 est.)
Gross Domestic Product (by sector): agriculture 6.3%, industry 21.1%, services 72.6% (2014 est.)
Government: republic
Languages: Arabic (official), French, English, Armenian

SOCIAL PROGRESS SNAPSHOT

Social Progress Index: 61.85 (+0.85 above/below 61 world average)
Basic Human Needs: 75.69 (+7.36 above/below 68.33 world average)
Foundations of Well-being: 65.89 (−0.56 above/below 66.45 world average)
Opportunity: 43.97 (−4.26 above/below 48.23 world average)

Following World War I, France acquired a mandate over Lebanon and granted this area independence in 1943. Since independence, the country has been marked by periods of political turmoil interspersed with prosperity built on finance and trade. Years of social and political instability followed the country's 1975–1990 civil war. Sectarianism is a key element of Lebanese political life. Neighboring Syria has historically influenced Lebanon's policies, and its military occupied Lebanon from 1976 until 2005. The Lebanon-based Hezbollah militia and Israel continued attacks against each other after Syria's withdrawal. Lebanon's borders with Syria and Israel remain unresolved.

Omanis in traditional garb gather in the streets of Muscat.

OMAN

QUICK STATS

Population: 3,286,936
Urban Population: 77.6% of total population (2015)
Comparative Size: twice the size of Georgia; slightly smaller than Kansas
Gross Domestic Product (per capita): $39,700 (2014 est.)
Gross Domestic Product (by sector): agriculture 1.3%, industry 55.2%, services 43.5% (2014 est.)
Government: monarchy
Languages: Arabic (official), English, Baluchi, Urdu, Indian dialects

SOCIAL PROGRESS SNAPSHOT

Foundations of Well-being: 70.47 (+4.02 above/below 66.45 world average)
(Not all scores computed due to data gaps in statistical sources.)

In the late 18th century, a newly established sultanate here signed the first in a series of friendship treaties with Britain. In 1970, Qaboos bin Said al Said overthrew his father, and has since ruled as sultan, but he has never designated a successor. His extensive modernization program has opened the country to the outside world while preserving long-standing close ties with the UK. Oman's moderate, independent foreign policy has sought to maintain good relations with all Middle Eastern countries.

QATAR

QUICK STATS
Population: 2,194,817 (2015 est.)
Urban Population: 99.2% of total population (2015)
Comparative Size: almost twice the size of Delaware; slightly smaller than Connecticut
Gross Domestic Product (per capita): $143,400 (2014 est.)
Gross Domestic Product (by sector): agriculture 0.1%, industr: 68%, services 31.9% (2014 est.)
Government: emirate
Languages: Arabic (official), English commonly used as a second language

SOCIAL PROGRESS SNAPSHOT
Foundations of Well-being: 70.60 (+4.15 above/below 66.45 world average)
Opportunity: 52.15 (+3.92 above/below 48.23 world average)
(Not all scores computed due to data gaps in statistical sources.)

Ruled by the Al Thani family since the1800s, Qatar transformed from a poor British protectorate to an oil-rich independent state. During the 1980s and early 1990s, the government under the emir siphoned off petroleum revenues and crippled the Qatari economy. Hamad bin Khalifa Al Thani overthrew his father in a bloodless coup in 1995. Hamad oversaw the creation of the pan-Arab news network Al Jazeera. In the 2000s, Qatar resolved its border disputes with both Bahrain and Saudi Arabia. In mid-2013 Hamad transferred power to his son, Tamim bin Hamad Al Thani. Emir Tamim has advocated for establishing advanced health care and education systems.

SAUDI ARABIA

QUICK STATS
Population: 27,752,316
Urban Population: 83.1% of total population (2015)
Comparative Size: slightly more than one-fifth the size of the US
Gross Domestic Product (per capita): $52,200 (2014 est.)
Gross Domestic Product (by sector): agriculture 2%, industry 59.7%, services 38.3% (2014 est.)
Government: parliamentary democracy
Language: Arabic (official)

SOCIAL PROGRESS SNAPSHOT
Social Progress Index: 64.27 (+3.27 above/below 61 world average)
Basic Human Needs: 82.87 (+14.54 above/below 68.33 world average)
Foundations of Well-being: 70.46 (+4.01 above/below 66.45 world average)
Opportunity: 39.49 (–8.74 above/below 48.23 world average)

Saudi Arabia is the birthplace of Islam and home to Islam's two holiest shrines in Mecca and Medina. The modern Saudi state was founded in 1932 after a 30-year campaign to unify most of the Arabian Peninsula. From 2005 to 2015, King Abdallah modernized the kingdom through a series of social and economic initiatives, including expanding employment and social opportunities for women. The Arab Spring inspired protests, and in response to unrest, King Abdallah announced a series of benefits for Saudi citizens in 2011, including funds to build affordable housing, salary increases for government workers, and unemployment entitlements. To promote increased political participation, the government held elections nationwide in 2011 for municipal councils, which hold little influence in the Saudi government. A growing population, aquifer depletion, and an economy largely dependent on petroleum are ongoing concerns.

SYRIA

QUICK STATS

Population: 17,064,854 (July 2014 est.)
Urban Population: 57.7% of total population (2015)
Comparative Size: slightly more than 1.5 times the size of Pennsylvania
Gross Domestic Product (per capita): $5,100 (2011 est.)
Gross Domestic Product (by sector): agriculture 16.4%, industry 22.7% services 60.9% (2014 est.)
Government: republic under an authoritarian regime
Languages: Arabic (official), Kurdish, Armenian, Aramaic, Circassian (widely understood); French, English (somewhat understood)

SOCIAL PROGRESS SNAPSHOT

Foundations of Well-being: 56.14 (-10.31 above/below 66.45 world average)
Opportunity: 24.25 (-23.98 above/below 48.23 world average)
(Not all scores computed due to data gaps in statistical sources.)

Following World War I, France took control over the province of Syria in the former Ottoman Empire. The French administered the area until granting it independence in 1946. The new country lacked political stability and experienced a series of military coups. Syria united with Egypt in February 1958 to form the United Arab Republic. In 1961 the two entities separated, and the Syrian Arab Republic was reestablished. In the 1967 Arab-Israeli War, Syria lost the Golan Heights region to Israel. In 1970 Hafiz al-Assad seized power and brought political stability to the country. After his death, his son, Bashar al-Assad, became president in 2000. Influenced by major uprisings in the region, antigovernment protests broke out starting in 2011. The government responded with a mix of military force and concessions. A truce brokered by the US and Russia went into effect in early 2016. So far, the conflict has displaced an estimated 12 million people, making the situation in Syria the largest humanitarian crisis in the world today.

UNITED ARAB EMIRATES

QUICK STATS

Population: 5,779,760
Urban Population: 85.5% of total population (2015)
Comparative Size: slightly larger than South Carolina; slightly smaller than Maine
Gross Domestic Product (per capita): $64,500 (2014 est.)
Gross Domestic Product (by sector): agriculture 0.6%, industry 58.9%, services 40.5% (2014 est.)
Government: federation with specified powers delegated to the UAE federal government and other powers reserved to member emirates
Languages: Arabic (official), Persian, English, Hindi, Urdu

SOCIAL PROGRESS SNAPSHOT

Social Progress Index: 72.79 (+11.79 above/below 61 world average)
Basic Human Needs: 89.63 (+21.30 above/below 68.33 world average)
Foundations of Well-being: 74.16 (+7.71 above/below 66.45 world average)
Opportunity: 54.59 (+6.36 above/below 48.23 world average)

In 1971 six states—Abu Dhabi, 'Ajman, Al Fujayrah, Ash Shariqah, Dubayy, and Umm al Qaywayn—merged to form the United Arab Emirates (UAE). They were joined in 1972 by Ra's al Khaymah. For more than three decades, oil and global finance drove the UAE's economy. However, in 2008–2009, falling oil prices, collapsing real estate prices, and the international banking crisis hit the UAE especially hard. The UAE has essentially avoided the Arab Spring unrest seen elsewhere in the Near East. In an effort to stem potential unrest, the government announced a $1.6 billion infrastructure investment plan and aggressively pursued political reform.

Conflict-affected people stand nearby their family rations provided by a local relief group, in Sana'a, Yemen. Almost nine in ten Yemenis face shortages of food and other vital supplies.

YEMEN

QUICK STATS

Population: 26,737,317 (2015 est.)
Urban Population: 34.6% of total population (2015)
Comparative Size: almost four times the size of Alabama; slightly larger than twice the size of Wyoming
Gross Domestic Product (per capita): $3,800 (2014 est.)
Gross Domestic Product (by sector): agriculture 9.2%; industry 26.8%; services 64% (2014 est.)
Government: republic
Language: Arabic (official)

SOCIAL PROGRESS SNAPSHOT

Social Progress Index: 40.30 (–20.70 above/below 61 world average)
Basic Human Needs: 49.72 (–18.61 above/below 68.33 world average)
Foundations of Well-being: 50.07 (–16.38 above/below 66.45 world average)
Opportunity: 21.12 (–27.11 above/below 48.23 world average)

North Yemen became independent from the Ottoman Empire in 1918. The British withdrew in 1967 from what became South Yemen. Three years later, the southern government adopted a Communist orientation. The massive exodus of hundreds of thousands of Yemenis from the south to the north contributed to two decades of hostility between the states. The two countries were formally unified as the Republic of Yemen in 1990. In 2000 Saudi Arabia and Yemen agreed to define their border. Fighting in the northwest between the government and the Huthis, a Shia minority, began in 2004 and has led to years of turmoil. The country consistently faces high unemployment, poor economic conditions, and corruption.

Egyptian fishermen collect fish from their nets in front of the new building of the Central Bank of Kuwait, in Kuwait. The Kuwaiti government has deposited $2 billion in the Central Bank of Egypt to support the country's economy.

CONCLUSION

As a whole, the Near East is a region that struggles for stability. Its history of religious conflict dates back thousands of years. The recent rise of the Islamic State (ISIS) and strife in Syria have created more turbulence. By the beginning of 2016, more than four million refugees have fled the region, seeking asylum in Europe and elsewhere.

Many countries in the Near East have authoritarian governments, meaning they favor the strict obedience to authority at the expense of personal freedom. When it comes to political rights and civil liberties, Freedom House (an organization that advocates for democracy, political freedom, and human rights) rates most countries in the region as not free or only partially free. Many in the Near East live in poverty, and the illiteracy rate is high. The area has been resistant to the ideals of democracy; however, many citizens in the region want democracy and personal freedoms, according to the Pew Research Center. For example, Pew has reported that solid majorities in Lebanon (84%), Turkey (71%), and Jordan (61%) have a "continuing desire for democracy."

In 2011, an attempt to move more toward democracy was seen throughout the region. Referred to after as the "Arab Spring," the period of time was marked by democratic uprisings in Syria, Yemen, Bahrain, Saudi Arabia, and Jordan, as well as several North African countries. These movements showed a public outcry for more freedom, more employment, better economies, and honest government. In many areas, a push toward democracy has sputtered to a halt, but there are a few bright spots. For example, parliamentary elections have been held in Iraq, and in Saudi Arabia in 2015, women were allowed for the first time to vote and to run for office in elections for municipal councils. Although tensions continue between Israel and Palestine, a large number of Palestinians live and work in Israel in peace and unity. Access to education in the Near East has improved, but the public education system is often strained with overcrowding and teachers who are overworked, poorly trained, and have inadequate materials.

In addition to the religious and political problems, water in the Near East has become increasingly scarce. Syria, Jordan, Iraq, and Iran have all seen growing "desertification"—more lands that were suitable for agriculture are disappearing. These are dire problems that must be addressed for future

Residents of Zanjan, Iran.

generations to survive in the region. Many nations in the area have relied on oil to support their economies, but countries such as the United States have become increasingly self-sufficient with regards to energy. A global shift in the reliance on Arab oil may force the region to look for other means to support their economies.

While the Near East as a whole may be inching toward a more progressive future, the process seems to be one of taking steps forward while also taking several steps back. There are certainly signs that many people of the Near East are striving toward a peaceful and productive future, but the road ahead is long. As US Vice President Joe Biden said, "The Middle East is hopeful. There is hope there."

Jordan's Queen Rania Al-Abdullah calls for the use of innovative tools in improving education as she visits Princess Taghreed School for Girls in Al Quwaismeh, Amman, Jordan.

Series Glossary

Anemia: a condition in which the blood doesn't have enough healthy red blood cells, most often caused by not having enough iron

Aquifer: an underground layer of water-bearing permeable rock, from which groundwater can be extracted using a water well

Asylum: protection granted by a nation to someone who has left their native country as a political refugee

Basic human needs: the things people need to stay alive: clean water, sanitation, food, shelter, basic medical care, safety

Biodiversity: the variety of life that is absolutely essential to the health of different ecosystems

Carbon dioxide (CO_2): a greenhouse gas that contributes to global warming and climate change

Censorship: the practice of officially examining books, movies, and other media and art, and suppressing unacceptable parts

Child mortality rate: the number of children that die before their fifth birthday for every 1,000 babies born alive

Communicable diseases: medical conditions spread by airborne viruses or bacteria or through bodily fluids such as malaria, tuberculosis, and HIV/AIDS; also called **infectious diseases;** differ from **noncommunicable diseases**, medical conditions not caused by infection and requiring long-term treatment such as diabetes or heart disease

Contraception: any form of birth control used to prevent pregnancy

Corruption: the dishonest behavior by people in positions of power for their own benefit

Deforestation: the clearing of trees, transforming a forest into cleared land

Desalination: a process that removes minerals (including salt) from ocean water

Discrimination: the unjust or prejudicial treatment of different categories of people, especially on the grounds of race, age, or sex

Ecosystem: a biological community of interacting organisms and their physical environment

Ecosystem sustainability: when we care for resources like clean air, water, plants, and animals so that they will be available to future generations

Emissions: the production and discharge of something, especially gas or radiation

Ethnicities: social groups that have a common national or cultural tradition

Extremism: the holding of extreme political or religious views; fanaticism

Famine: a widespread scarcity of food that results in malnutrition and starvation on a large scale

Food desert: a neighborhood or community with no walking access to affordable, nutritious food

Food security: having enough to eat at all times

Greenhouse gas emissions: any of the atmospheric gases that contribute to the greenhouse effect by absorbing infrared radiation produced by solar warming of the earth's surface. They include carbon dioxide (CO_2), methane (CH_4), nitrous oxide (NO_2), and water vapor.

Gross domestic product (GDP): the total value of all products and services created in a country during a year

GDP per capita (per person): the gross domestic product divided by the number of people in the country. For example, if the GDP for a country is one hundred million dollars ($100,000,000) and the population is one million people (1,000,000), then the GDP per capita (value created per person) is $100.

Habitat: environment for a plant or animal, including climate, food, water, and shelter

Incarceration: the condition of being imprisoned

Income inequality: when the wealth of a country is spread very unevenly among the population

Indigenous people: culturally distinct groups with long-standing ties to the land in a specific area

Inflation: when the same amount money buys less from one day to the next. Just because things cost more does not mean that people have more money. Low-income people trapped in a high inflation economy can quickly find themselves unable to purchase even the basics like food.

Infrastructure: permanent features required for an economy to operate such as transportation routes and electric grids; also systems such as education and courts

Latrine: a communal outdoor toilet, such as a trench dug in the ground

Literate: able to read and write

Malnutrition: lack of proper nutrition, caused by not having enough to eat, not eating enough of the right things, or being unable to use the food that one does eat

Maternal mortality rate: the number of pregnant women who die for every 100,000 births.

Natural resources: industrial materials and assets provided by nature such as metal deposits, timber, and water

Nongovernmental organization (NGO): a nonprofit, voluntary citizens' group organized on a local, national, or international level. Examples include organizations that support human rights, advocate for political participation, and work for improved health care.

Parliament: a group of people who are responsible for making the laws in some kinds of government

Prejudice: an opinion that isn't based on facts or reason

Preventive care: health care that helps an individual avoid illness

Primary school: includes grades 1–6 (also known as elementary school); precedes **secondary** and **tertiary education**, schooling beyond the primary grades; secondary generally corresponds to high school, and tertiary generally means college-level

Privatization: the transfer of ownership, property, or business from the government to the private sector (the part of the national economy that is not under direct government control)

Sanitation: conditions relating to public health, especially the provision of clean drinking water and adequate sewage disposal

Stereotypes: are common beliefs about the nature of the members of a specific group that are based on limited experience or incorrect information

Subsistence agriculture: a system of farming that supplies the needs of the farm family without generating any surplus for sale

Surface water: the water found above ground in streams, lakes, and rivers

Tolerance: a fair, objective, and permissive attitude toward those whose opinions, beliefs, practices, racial or ethnic origins, and so on differ from one's own

Trafficking: dealing or trading in something illegal

Transparency: means that the government operates in a way that is visible to and understood by the public

Universal health care: a system in which every person in a country has access to doctors and hospitals

Urbanization: the process by which towns and cities are formed and become larger as more and more people begin living and working in central areas

Well-being: the feeling people have when they are healthy, comfortable, and happy

Whistleblower: someone who reveals private information about the illegal activities of a person or organization

Index

RESOURCES

Continue exploring the world of development through this assortment of online and print resources. Follow links, stay organized, and maintain a critical perspective. Also, seek out news sources from outside the country in which you live.

Websites

Social Progress Imperative: socialprogressimperative.org
United Nations—Human Development Indicators: hdr.undp.org/en/countries and Sustainable Development Goals: un.org/sustainabledevelopment/sustainable-development-goals
World Bank—World Development Indicators: data.worldbank.org/data-catalog/world-development-indicators
World Health Organization—country statistics: who.int/gho/countries/en
U.S. State Department—human rights tracking site: humanrights.gov/dyn/countries.html
Oxfam International: oxfam.org/en
Amnesty International: amnesty.org/en
Human Rights Watch: hrw.org
Reporters without Borders: en.rsf.org
CIA—The World Factbook: cia.gov/library/publications/the-world-factbook

Books

Literary and classics
The Good Earth, Pearl S. Buck
Grapes of Wrath, John Steinbeck
The Jungle, Upton Sinclair

Nonfiction—historical/classic
Angela's Ashes, Frank McCourt
Lakota Woman, Mary Crow Dog with Richard Erdoes
Orientalism, Edward Said
Silent Spring, Rachel Carson
The Souls of Black Folk, W.E.B. Du Bois

Nonfiction: development and policy—presenting a range of views
Behind the Beautiful Forevers: Life, Death, and Hope in a Mumbai Undercity, Katherine Boo
The Bottom Billion: Why the Poorest Countries Are Failing and What Can Be Done About It, Paul Collier
The End of Poverty, Jeffrey D. Sachs
For the Common Good: Redirecting the Economy toward Community, the Environment, and a Sustainable Future, Herman E. Daly
I Am Malala: The Girl Who Stood Up for Education and Was Shot by the Taliban, Malala Yousafzai and Christina Lamb
The Life You Can Save: Acting Now to End World Poverty, Peter Singer
Mismeasuring Our Lives: Why GDP Doesn't Add Up, Joseph E. Stiglitz, Amartya Sen, and Jean-Paul Fitoussi
Rachel and Her Children: Homeless Families in America, Jonathan Kozol
The White Man's Burden: Why the West's Efforts to Aid the Rest Have Done So Much Ill and So Little Good, William Easterly

Foreword writer Michael Green is an economist, author, and cofounder of the Social Progressive Imperative. A UK native and graduate of Oxford University, Green has worked in aid and development for the British government and taught economics at Warsaw University.

Author Don Rauf has written more than 30 nonfiction books, mostly for children and young adults, including *Killer Lipstick and Other Spy Gadgets*, *The Rise and Fall of the Ottoman Empire*, and *Simple Rules for Card Games*. He lives in Seattle with his wife, Monique, and son, Leo.